Tricky Riddles
FOR SMART KIDS

333 DIFFICULT BUT FUN RIDDLES AND BRAIN
TEASERS FOR KIDS AND FAMILIES (AGES 8-12)

JORDAN MOORE

ISBN: 979-8-88768-017-0

Contents

✧ Introduction ✧

What sets humans apart from computers? After all, many computers can process answers at a remarkable rate. What is human intelligence? And more importantly, how can we encourage the unique ways of problem-solving that we as humans are capable of?

Tricky Riddles for Smart Kids is a book that creates challenges in order to expand this very intelligence. This book takes the reader on a journey to learn about four Smart Kids from around the globe. In these stories, we follow Alex, Ilene, Zachary, and Jonelle as they tell us all about where they are from as well as their favorite subjects.

We live in a time where practically everything we are to learn in schools can be googled. The most incredible thing about a riddle is that very often the answer can be right in front of you, calling you to piece it together. Many varieties of riddles exist, and as the readers find themselves immersed in the lives of Alex, Ilene, Zachary, and Jonelle, they will begin to see patterns emerge.

You may find that different types of rhymes or riddles speak to you while others may speak to other people. Suddenly, the reader finds solutions but comes away with new friends and connections. These books are designed with family and friends in mind as it may take multiple minds to be able to solve some of these more challenging riddles.

If you decide to set forth on the journey of learning about the remarkable lives of these four Smart Kids, you will find yourself working to make sense of the seemingly senseless, providing new reason only to be met with further developments, and asking questions that simply produce more questions. In time, however, you just might be met with answers.

For what do you call a life that lives to tell tales of overcoming? A life that decides to open the door and make its way to new horizons?

Chapter 1

Meet Alex

✦✦ Chapter 1: Meet Alex ✦✦

Before we have the opportunity to meet our good friend Alex, we are first going to have to solve some riddles to find out just who Alex is! In order to solve the first clue, you just might need to find someone who knows a bit of science.

You've known its name since kindergarten, maybe even before. Alex holds a hint at the end of his name. My mother has two. My sister has two. My father and I have one. Alex only has one. What do we have?

Hint 1: What do we need to learn about Alex?
Hint 2: Chromosome

If you flip me upside down, I remain the same. If you tilt me to the side, the meaning becomes greatly changed. What am I?

Hint 1: What do we need to learn about Alex?
Hint 2: What age is Alex?

Way to go, Smart Kids! Let's see what else we can learn about our friend, Alex. The next three riddles provide us with clues about where Alex is from.

I am eaten boiled or steamed
As part of a main meal
I can also be Krispie
In a breakfast cereal

{4}
I'm a transport you don't have to drive
Which means you can sit back and relax
I can take you across the country
Not in the air but along some tracks

{5}
You may see me on a phone, console, or tv,
A very popular one's name is Eevee,
Our mascot is yellow,
Who travels with a fellow

Time to put it all together — Where is Alex from?

{6}
You've had three clues to help,
To find where I spend my days
A land that is full of kelp,
And advanced robotic ways

Konnichiwa! My name is Alex, and I am 8 years old. I live in Okinawa, Japan. Japan is known for having the fastest train in the world clocking in at 374 miles per hour. See if you can solve the next few riddles to learn about my favorite things.

{7}
You may play me in your home
I'm on screens up high and in hand
2D, 3D, wherever you may roam
I can show you every type of land.

{8}
You love me, you hate me,
It makes no difference to me
I come in all flavors, portions, and styles
Grown to meet everyone's needs.

9

I travel along the water
My master is the wind
I catch it, it propels me
Unless I need a mend.

I spend my summer days playing video games, eating tasty foods, and sailing. See if you can solve these riddles and learn more about my family. The next three Riddles 10, 11, and 12 will provide clues to what my dad does for a living.

 10

I am safe when home,
until you take me out
My friends look like me,
but they have a spout
My life can be in danger,
If there ever is a drought.

 11

Only by reading a certain way may you
Know where you begin,
I'm a name you may
Not know,
A city in Japan,
Where ocean surrounds
All.

 12

I use a net, hook, and line.
Where I work changes every day,
I wait with patience every time,
And so, they come this way
What am I?

My father is a well-known fisherman in Okinawa. Our family's fishing business goes back generations, even as far back as the Edo period in the early 17th century. I am very excited to share some riddles with you. One of my father's favorite pastimes while fishing is asking me to solve his riddles. In Japan, we have many riddles that deal with play on words in the Japanese language. There are many rhymes that deal with a play on words in English as well. See if you can solve these.

13
I can take you here or there, I can stand on my own,
I never will tire, but at times I am two-tired. What am I?

Hint 1: Is there a word that has any double meaning?
Hint 2: I am something that is a favorite way to get around in Japan.

14
I see you at the beginning, though my eyes may never see your end. What am I?

Hint 1: Sometimes riddles give you the answer right away
Hint 2: This surrounds Japan.

Some riddles are all about misdirection. If you find yourself getting carried away with the details, you may have forgotten an important hint from the beginning. Something that helps me solve riddles that are trying to distract me is writing down all the information I know.

15 I rode on the bullet train to Tokyo, Japan. I bought a bowl of ramen and a new shirt. What did I buy first?

Hint 1: Is something distracting you?
Hint 2: I am purchased every day by a majority of Japanese people.

> **Again try to write down elements of the riddle and see if any patterns emerge. Sometimes riddles have a visual component.**

16 Ten fish I caught without an eye,
and nine without a tail.
Half of eight, and six missing heads,
landed in my pail.
Who can tell me,
as I ask it,
how many fish are in my basket?

> **The next few riddles are about my mother. Sometimes we can even use Google to gain further insight into the clues the riddles offer us.**

17 A land of hot dogs
Wolves, bears, and moose
And cabins made from logs
Movies, music, footloose
Traffic, traffic, to get to jobs

18 The job of a mother's father
Green for Red, White, and Blue
A base located in another
Land that enjoys monkfish stew

19

Now a mother working
Trying to save lives
After years of learning
How to work special knives

My mother was raised at the Okinawa military base. She is American. I have visited America in the summer many times, but this summer my father is going to take me on his fishing boat in Okinawa. My mother is a doctor who works in a local hospital and cares for Okinawa locals. You now know a bit about my parents as well as some of my favorite hobbies. One hobby, though, solving riddles and puzzles. For the next riddles, you can learn more about me and some more of my favorite things.

20

You may sing in songs you can move me
In your effort to win over someone you love
The time it takes for me to move and shift
A significantly noticeable nudge
I will already be gone from your perirhinal
With your eyes that can no longer budge

21

Red, orange, and yellow
Green, blue, and violet.
You hope to see a pot and fellow
But as you peer through the horizon
You never see the end of it.

{22}

I started out on rocks, markings etched across cave walls.
Now you see me everywhere from your favorite clothes
To packaged foods, and even by your own two hands.
Framed now in your home on your very walls

{23}

You come here to learn
To listen, see, and play
I have many doors
I have many windows
To learn about out there
Here, I have you stay.

{24}

If I run across this line.
An eruption will begin
If I do so before you
Then I get to say I win

{25}

I have multiple names
I come inside a box
I may have a deck, or dice, or pawns
Or a map of fantastical lands
And inspire fun talks

{26}

You build me with chairs and poles
Really with whatever you can find
A castle or a ship, I take on many roles
Covering me in blankets
Is how you spend your time

27

There is air here

I raise my arms above my head

There is no air here

My legs move back and forth

There is air here

I curl up in a roll and push

There is no air here

I love building forts, swimming, and going to school. I also love drawing, playing board games, and looking at scenic mountains and at rainbows after it rains. But I really love sitting around and solving puzzles and riddles too. Some riddles have to do with finding patterns. See if you can find the patterns in these riddles.

28

A dog, cat, and rat decided to share a meal together. They each brought the following

Dog: *I'm bringing cheese*

Cat: *I'm bringing rice*

Rat: *I'm bringing donuts*

Dog: *Acorns*

Cat: *Alfalfa*

Rat: *Onions*

Dog: *Tator-Tots*

Cat: *Tacos*

Rat: *and I'll also be bringing grapes*

What is the pattern?

Alex's grandfather has five grandchildren. The eldest's name is Jana. Next is Jene, then Jini, and Jono. What is the last grandchild's name?

 If 2 is 8

A train at 4

While 0 is 16

A race to 24

Leaves us where at 23?

Wow! You're really good at solving riddles. Now you know a lot about me. I want to take you on an adventure to one of my favorite things to do next!

✦ *Chapter 1: Answers* ✦

1. The 'X' chromosome. You learn the alphabet in kindergarten. The end of Alex is x. Therefore, we learn that Alex is male.

2. Eight. The number stays the same when you flip it upside down, but if you tilt it to the side, it makes the infinity symbol: ∞

3. Rice.

4. Train.

5. Pokémon. Eevee is a yellow Pokémon species. Ash is the boy (fellow) who collects Pokémon.

6. Japan.

7. Video games.

8. Food.

9. Sailboat.

10. Fish. Fish are safe in water until taken out. Fish don't have a spout, but other friendly sea creatures do. Fish can be harmed in times of drought.

11. Okinawa.

12. Fisherman.

13. Bike. Bikes never get tired, but they do often have two tires.

14. The sea. "See" sounds like "sea."

15. Train ticket. Before you board the train, you need to buy a ticket!

16. Zero—10 without the "I" is 0, 9 without its tail leaves 0, 8 ← divided here leaves two 0s, 6 without its head leaves a 0.

17. America. Being "footloose" means being free.

18. Alex's grandfather worked for a US military base in Okinawa, Japan.

19. Doctor. Doctors, particularly surgeons, learn how to use special knives to perform surgeries.

20. Mountains. "Move mountains" is a common saying, but in reality, it takes a long time for mountains to gradually shift their position.

21. Rainbow. "Pot and fellow" refers to the leprechaun and his pot of gold said to be found at the end of a rainbow.

22. Drawings.

23. School.

24. Race. The line is the start line. If you cross the line too early, the other racer will win.

25. Board games.

26. Homemade forts.

27. Swimming. Humans need to come up for air.

28. Dog spells Cat. Cat spells Rat. Rat spells Dog.

29. Alex. He is his grandfather's grandchild too!

30. School. The answer to the 2nd riddle is 8, train is the answer to the fourth, 0 is #16, race is #24, and the answer to "leave us where at 23" refers to riddle number 23... school!

Chapter 2

Video Games

✦ Chapter 2: Video Games ✦

These riddles are about video games. I love video games. Do you have favorite video game characters? I do. Have you ever wondered how video games are made? I have. Do you enjoy solving puzzles in video games? Me too! These next riddles have everything to do with some of my favorite characters and stories in video games. If you have friends or parents who play video games, have them join you for some riddle fun.

{31} When I'm last the power of lighting finds me,
Sometimes a bullet ride can pull me through
When I'm first I'm left with nothing but shells
I guess sometimes I can get some banana peels too.

{32} I like to take my time, as I beautify the land,
I take on debts to build something new.
But I can also spend time in the sand
Fishing, mining, and bugs to pursue
Planting flowers at my whim,
With no serious demands
By Nook, Tommy, or Tim

{33} I am the original nemesis
To a carpenter turned red hat plumber
But I forgot my life of cruelness
In favor of the country's summer
Now my family and I can rest
Until the land freezes over
And together fix the theft

{34} Mario, Donkey Kong, and Sonic the Hedgehog are at the park playing catch. Mario and Donkey Kong are throwing the ball back and forth. Who is Sonic playing catch with?

{35} What do fish, birds, and Pac-Man have in common?

{36} I am reborn time and time again
Each time to save the day
I travel far and wide to win
Meeting many along the way
Each link creates more canon
All to defeat the great Ganon

{37} I am a colorful puzzle of pieces
I come in four cubes all arranged differently
You can speed me up but can't slow me down
And if you don't find where the pieces fit,
you lose.

{38} You explore me endlessly
Some fly, some walk
But all decide to build
And some never stop
Until the world is made
In the image that they choose

{39} You swing and hit the ball
But your walls never feel it bounce
If you swing and you fall
You still will have a chance
A flick of the wrist is all
It takes to still be able to advance

You meet new friends and capture them
You hold them in your pocket
Until you need them to help you
Defeat that darn Team Rocket

Those were some of my favorite characters and games I've ever played. But have you ever wondered how video games are made? My uncle does the coding for video games, and he explained it in a letter he wrote me. I'll read some for you.

Most games are coded using C++. This style of coding focuses on objects and coding that tells how those objects move in relation to the space that they are in. So, any time you move your video game character, a series of codes are processing that movement in real-time based on the rules created for that character! And the rules of the space! The very first program used on computers was a program written in binary. That means two symbols were used to create a certain meaning. A series of 0's and 1's could translate into saying "HELLO". You can think of binary as an old language that computers used to use before they became more advanced.

So, to honor our video games ancestors, I have riddles for you that are all about numbers!

{41} My mom has four brothers playing video games and each of them have a sister who also plays video games. How many children play video games in my mom's family?

{42} A video game controller and a new game cost $130. The controller costs $100 more than the video game. How much does the controller cost?

{43} How many times can you take 1 out of 10?

{44} What is the next number in the pattern?

4, 7, 13, 25, ___

{45} Alex and his friend are going to play virtual golf. They spend half of their money on tickets, $10 on food, and $5 each for virtual costumes. How much did a ticket to virtual golf cost if they have no more money?

{46} What is the next number in this pattern?

11, 10, 101, 100, 1001, 1000, 10001, 10000, 100001, _____

{47} You arrived at the final boss. It takes 4,000 hit points to defeat him. Your attacks do 30 points of hit damage. The boss can heal themselves 500 points for every 10 minutes of real-time gameplay. It takes you 30 minutes to defeat him. How many hit points does it take to defeat the final boss?

{48} Alex made his way to the arcade. On his way to the arcade, he met a boy with six friends, and each of them had one dog. How many were going to the arcade?

49 If 3+11+9 =10, what does 100+19+8=

50 If 40=5, 5=4, 4=4, 82=9, what does 8=?

Video games are like riddles. Through trial and error, you learn about the rules of the game. Then you piece together the pattern. Sometimes video games have rules like our world, and sometimes the rules are different. You don't see your sister running as fast as Sonic or your brother creating electricity like Pikachu.

51 In Minecraft, you can play Creative Mode and fly around. Or you can play Survival mode, and the law of gravity is the rule. However, that rule only affects your player. Therefore, how do you create a floating island in Survival mode if all you can do is build and destroy blocks?

52 Who would be the winner of a match between Mario, Sonic, and Pikachu?

53 In the videogame Pikmin, you control stranded Captain Omar, who finds an alien species called Pikmin. The game uses color coding as well as imbuing special abilities on each of the Pikmin to set you up to solve various puzzles. What is the main puzzle you are trying to solve?

Hint: The answer is in the riddle

54 You are playing a 2D game that involves running away from a monster. Which way do you run?

55 You're driving your car, and you come upon a marching band of mice in the middle of the road with broken instruments. They are not moving. What do you do to get them to move?

56 Ekans, Venemoth, and Eevee are in a Pokémon battle. Who wins?

57 You're playing Mario Party as Princess Peach, and you are 10 spaces from the star. How many dice rolls with a pentagonal trapezohedron does it take to get to the star?

58 What is the common pattern of the below words?

Coins, Cheap, Gonna, Kiln

59 Which character name should be changed in the pattern below to make the pattern correct?

1) Mario   : Peach
2) Bowser : Link
3) Sonic   : Bowser
4) Peach   : Mario
5) Zelda   : Peach
6) Mario   : Peach
7) Bowser : Bowser
8) Sonic   : Mario
9) Peach   : Peach
10) Zelda   : Link
11) Mario   : Bowser
12) Bowser : Mario

60

I have spikes but don't use them as weapons
I'm faster rolling than I am running
A man with an egg-shaped head likes to threaten
Me, but I tend to leave him fuming

61

Mario and his friends were hanging out
Mario needed a moment, so he sat
His friends continued along on their route

Mario couldn't join them as he was _____

✧ Chapter 2: Answers ✦

31. Mario Kart. The riddle refers to powers and obstacles in the game.

32. Animal Crossing. The riddle describes the game-play.

33. Donkey Kong. Nemesis means enemy.

34. Himself.

35. Humans feed them pellets.

36. Link from Legend of Zelda.

37. Tetris.

38. Minecraft.

39. Wii Sports.

40. Pokémon.

41. 5. All of the brothers have 1 sister (Alex's mother); all 5 play.

42. $15. The game costs $115.

43. Once. Because it would no longer be 10.

44. 49. Each # is doubled minus 1.

45. Tickets cost $10. They started with $40. 40-half= 20 − 10= (2x5) = 0.

46. 100000 - the numbers follow a clear pattern.

47. It takes 4,000 damage points.

48. One. Only Alex was going to the arcade.

49. It equals 1. Because the first letter of the word form of the numerical number spells the answers. 10: T(3) E(11) N(9).

50. It equals 5. The answers refer to the number of letters in the number.

51. While you have to obey the law of gravity, the blocks you create don't. You can create it in a number of ways via stairs/scaffolding that you then can destroy afterward.

52. Any of them. It depends on who is the best at Super Smash Brothers.

53. Omar is stranded. The main puzzle you are solving is how to get Omar home.

54. Forward. 2D games only allow you to move forward or backward. If you're running away, you would only be able to move forward.

55. Turn the radio on so they have music to march to.

56. Eevee wins because the riddle spells EVE by the first letter of the names of the Pokémon.

57. As few as 1 or as many as 10. As it is a 10-sided dice.

58. They are all anagrams of character names from video games: Sonic, Peach, Ganon, Link.

59. 6 needs to be changed to Mario: Link. The pattern falls vertically. The left being Mario, Bowser, Sonic, Peach, Zelda. The right being Peach, Link, Bowser, Mario.

60. Sonic the Hedgehog.

61. Flat. 2D images have to move linearly whereas 3D games allow the characters to move openly through the world. Mario is depicted 2D and therefore he is flat while the rest of the characters are 3D.

Chapter 3

Food

✦ Chapter 3: Food ✦

It was so fun talking about video games! One of my other favorite things to do every day is to eat tasty food. What is your favorite kind of food? Do you like to eat fish? We eat lots of fish in Japan as well as seaweed. We have seaweed salad, sushi, nori, and also snack on salted dried seaweed like chips! I like to take the dried seaweed and grab a handful of sticky rice and gobble it up. I like learning about different kinds of foods from all over the world. I also have a lot of favorite foods I eat anytime I can. I sometimes cook with my mom too. Do you ever cook with your parents? Grab someone who likes food and see if you can figure out these fun food riddles.

 I choke on art.

 What ingredient is missing from this list?

Salad: Avocado, Lettuce, Sour cream, Arugula

 First part is force. Second part is family.

 I have three letters in my name.
But you need to double the number of letters to spell me.

 You say the same thing twice when there are two of me.

 What do the below words have in common?

Aunt, melon, mile, beard, fires

{68} I find myself blue, my voice raspy, and I have to drink slowly using a straw. Do you have anything you recommend for my ailments?

{69} What similarity is there between soybeans, chickpeas, and wheat?

{70} What do these have in common?

Peas, beans, peppers

{71} What is Step 5 in the recipe?

Step 1. Boil the potatoes.

Step 2. Add salt

Step 3. Keep stirring as you boil

Step 4. Empty out the water and mash

{72} If you want to keep me longer
You can leave me in the sun
If you like my flavor to be stronger
You can crush me, it's quite fun.
Boil me with sugar, in case you were
To have a ton.

{73} A Ghoul was feeling Hungary,
Asking for his favorite dish,
What do you serve him?

74 What do you call an English cow who has fallen into a fire?

75 My name starts with soda
But it isn't an ingredient.
I hail from Ireland
But they don't knead me.

76 I am sheep stomach. But to know my name,
you need an old lady. And the second thing
you need is to add the beginning of gist
Which is the gist of the riddle.

77 What do you think that all these foods have in common?

Bread, cheese, soy sauce, and sour cream

78 I am fried, I am mashed, I am wedged

79 You can find me on a calendar.
You can put me in a smoothie.
You can take me to your prom.
What am I?

80 Sometimes I am a side dish.
You can dip in me if you prefer
Sometimes I have meat or fish
Ouch, I'm hot, check my temperature,
Before you take a bite, add garnish
I can be clear or creamy too.
When you're sick make me rich
It will help with the common flu.

{81} I am a group.
As different as can be,
but if you forget two
Try to enjoy at least three.
An apple, carrot, and milk will do
At least just for a snack
Before bedtime though, will you?
Try something from the entire pack!

{82} I'm another word for crazy.

Squirrels go _____ for me.
You'll find me in a tree

{83} Finish the riddle

Made with milk and ice cream
I'm stirred into a frozen dream
It may taste as good as cake

As I am a yummy

{84} What is missing from these numbers?

$$\tfrac{1}{4} = 4 = 12 = 2$$

{85} Finish the riddle

I pull out my peanut butter
I spread it on my bread
I make some for my brother

Until we are both well

I am extremely sweet
But you might say gross
As I am made,
even though I am a treat
For when I am found,
you'll hear quite the sound,
as you comb through to eat

What is the similarity to all these words?

Toss, beat, whip, stir, blend

You add eggs, flour, olive, salt.
You form me in whatever way you choose
You dry me on a rack or in the oven.
Then boil me when you're ready to use

Diced, chopped, minced.
Even though you have the knife
It's you who's going to cry.

I am part tree and part fruit.

I am made up of three most commonly

+

But you really only need two to be fed

+

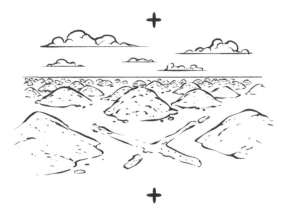

+

Patience is key to my rise in quality

+

Whether thinly sliced or nicely spread
What am I?

62. Artichoke. See how you can re-arrange the phrase to get the answer?

63. Salsa. The first letter of each item spells "salsa".

64. Pumpkin (pump + kin). Kin is another word for family.

65. Banana (repeat A and N).

66. Pear. A pair of pears.

67. They are all anagrams for a type of food: Tuna, Lemon, Lime, Bread, Fries.

68. Prescribe them with blueberries, raspberries, and strawberries.

69. They are all types of flours.

70. They all come in green.

71. B A K E is the first letter in every step. Bake the potatoes.

72. Grapes turn into raisins in the sun. The flavor can be stronger when crushed to make juice. You can also make jam.

73. Goulash – the national dish of Hungary is Goulash.

74. Roast beef. Which is the national dish of England.

75. Soda bread is a type of bread that doesn't need kneading.

76. Haggis is sheep stomach, and it is a well-known Scottish pudding.

77. They are all fermented foods.

78. Potatoes. These are all different ways to prepare and serve this vegetable.

79. A date. The word has multiple meanings: a specific day, a type of fruit, or someone you ask out.

80. Soup. It is often served to someone who is unwell.

81. The food groups. The five food groups are fruits, vegetables, grains, protein, and dairy in the USA.

82. Nuts.

83. Milkshake.

84. Measurements. A 1/4 cup equals 4 tablespoons, which equals 23 teaspoons, which lastly equals 2 ounces.

85. Fed.

86. Honey. The sound referred to is the bees when honey is taken from their hives.

87. They each are used as cooking terms for mixing.

88. Pasta.

89. Onion. Have you ever cried while preparing an onion?

90. Pineapple (pine tree + apple fruit).

91. Bread. Bread typically has three ingredients (flour, water, and yeast), but you can just use flour and water.

Chapter 4

Aquatic Life

Chapter 4: Aquatic Life

I love the ocean. I'm lucky that I see it every day. My dad takes me sailing. He's loved the ocean longer than me. He often tells tales of the sea. Sometimes it's nice to stare across the water as we wait to catch a fish. He asks me so many riddles! I try to talk in rhymes when I can so that I can make riddles of my own one day. Do you ever write your own riddles? It's super fun. You should try to make some up about the sea.

92

Part of me is known for being funny
Though one interpretation has been serious
I'm mainly two colors and no, I'm not the one with the big red nose

93

I travel with my home
It sits upon my back
Sometimes when I'm scared
I crawl into my shell.
But then I remember my anemones
That protect me from my enemies

94

I am a million tiny specks
Formed through years of waves
Crashing against my shores

95

I have four arms and four legs.
Or maybe it was two arms and six legs.
I have no bones.
I squish my way through holes

I am a predator
From underneath the waves
So, when you hear the
Da dum Da dum
You swim away in fear

I am the thing that happens
When you tilt your hand
Back and forth.
Or I crash on top of the sand
And recede till I'm
Quickly out of reach.

The moon controls my current
Sending me in and out of depths
Breaking up the coastline
And causing me unrest

Within my home, great secrets I hold
Open me up and the truth shall be told
I typically drift, forgotten by most
Floating along 'til I find a new coast
And if I do perish before I am found
My existence is meaningless, my purpose is drowned
I'll wither away amongst the debris
My secret decayed so no one shall see
What am I?

{100}
I come from inside
I come from outside
I come from the sky
I come from the ground
What am I?

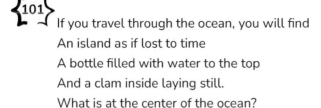

101 If you travel through the ocean, you will find
An island as if lost to time
A bottle filled with water to the top
And a clam inside laying still.
What is at the center of the ocean?

102 My first is in first
My second in nine
My third in oyster
My fourth in urchin
What am I?

103 I spend most of my time where I am slow
I'm fast where I cannot breathe
I am opposite the scenery
If you were here, you'd probably leave
What am I?

104 I am a lost city in the Atlantic Sea.
Just change one single letter
And you will have me

105 Add an e and d to poison.
And a gift from Ariel's father
And you would find
The mystical weapon of the sea

106 What do you get when you add water to a scary movie?

107
I am a tool.
But I didn't intend to be.
I just have different views.

108
Sally sells seashells by the seashore
But Sally let out a shrill as she came down the hill from a thrill
And so Sally sold no more.
What made Sally stop selling?

109
I am a mythical creature known for my sound
I have scales but am not a dragon
And have yet to be found.

110
I happen when I am too afraid to speak
I happen after I've had a fever
You get me when you dig for me

111
The first word keeps you safe behind a door
The second word keeps baby birds safe
The third word refers to creatures that frighten you

112
You eat me with peanut butter
But don't swim with me unless
You want to get so badly stung
You'll need a whole week to rest.

113
I wash your dishes.
I'm on your TV.
I absorb
I'm from the ocean floor

I'm not an X-ray, a sun ray, or a freeze ray, I am a?

 I live in water but I breathe
I eat tiny plankton though I'm huge
I can't speak in the air but I can blow
What am I?

 I'm a fish but I am a celebrity
I'm in the sky and ocean
But my tight grip won't let me fall.
What am I?

 I can get pregnant but I am not a mom
I am a horse but I cannot gallop on the land
What am I?

 I'm born with my skeleton on the outside
But don't worry, it lets me hide away
I can outlive you and your children
I need to be outside on a sunny day

 What kind of fish coddles its kids?

 I am in most of your body but you don't see me.
I cover the world but most people don't see me.
Without me, you would die.
Without you, I would thrive.

{121} What is the commonality between these two men?

92. Clownfish. Some clowns are funny, others are serious. Clownfish are orange and white.

93. A hermit crab. A hermit crab lives symbiotically with anemones who keep predators at bay.

94. Beaches. The tiny specks are sand. Beaches are formed by waves crashing against land over many years.

95. Octopus. They have eight legs total.

96. Shark. "Da dum Da dum" refers to the theme music of the famous shark movie, Jaws.

97. Waves. Two meanings of "wave": a gesture you make with your hand and water formations in the sea.

98. Ocean. A stormy ocean is not calm = unrest.

99. A message in a bottle. Debris is scattered rubbish or remains. If the paper in the bottle is destroyed by water, the message is lost.

100. Water. Humans have water in their bodies. Water also comes from outside our bodies, from the sky and up from the ground.

101. The CEA because the center of the word ocean is CEA.

102. Fish. First letter is F in first. Second letter I in nine. Third is in the S and the fourth is the H in Heaven.

103. Penguin. Penguins are slow on land but fast in the ocean, though they cannot breathe underwater. They are typically found in places without much vegetation (scenery), mainly Antarctica—a very cold and inhospitable place for humans!

104. Atlantis. Atlantic minus C and plus S= Atlantis.

105. The trident of Poseidon. Ariel's father in The Little Mermaid has a magical trident.

106. A sea monster. Scary movies often have monsters, so when you add water, you have a sea monster.

107. A hammerhead shark. A hammer is a tool, but to a hammerhead shark, it's just the shape of their head.

108. She fell ill. "Ill" rhymes with "shrill," "hill," and "thrill".

109. Mermaid. Mermaids are known for their beautiful singing and have scales on their tales. But are mermaids real? We haven't found one yet!

110. You clam up when scared. Your skin is clammy when you sweat out a fever, and you get clams by digging.

111. A lock keeps you safe, a nest keeps baby birds safe, monsters frighten you. Lock Nest Monster = Loch Ness Monster.

112. Jellyfish. Peanut butter and jelly. Jellyfish can sting you with their tentacles, which can be poisonous.

113. Sponges wash dishes. SpongeBob's on TV. Sponges absorb, and they are from the ocean floor.

114. A stingray.

115. Whale. Whales can breathe underwater and make sounds by blowing through their blowholes.

116. A starfish. Celebrities are also known as "stars". Stars are in the sky; fish are in the ocean. Starfish are good at gripping onto things.

117. A seahorse. Male seahorses can get pregnant.

118. A turtle. Turtles' shells are skeletons. Turtles live for a very long time and like to bask in the sun.

119. A cod.

120. Water. Humans have water in their bodies. Lots of people live in landlocked areas, so never see the ocean. Humans need water to live but if there were no humans, bodies of water would be fuller and less polluted.

121. They are both stepping. One man is step dancing and the other is stepping the mast.

✳ **Chapter 5** ✳

Meet Ilene

✦ Chapter 5: Meet Ilene ✦

Before we meet Ilene, it's important to understand how riddles work across the globe. Many cultures have riddles. Many riddles cannot translate to our language because the riddle has to do with wordplay. In someone else's language, they may utilize the same word to mean two different things, but in our language, we use two distinct words. See if you can solve the riddles below so you can learn more about Ilene and where she is from. Invite someone you know who loves words and enjoys expanding their vocabulary to help out. While you can't find the answer by searching the internet, the internet can still help us get closer to solving the riddle.

My beloved has called me a sycophant
As I praise her boss incessantly
However, the meaning changes in my land
I chuckle and say awkwardly
"I am no snitch" as I take a bite
of my ripe fig to which I delight
at my joke that only I find funny

What land is this man from?

Hint 1: If you struggled with this riddle, the next three riddles provide clues.

I was called the third but known as great
I commanded the largest empire of ancient times
I share part of my name to one you will find
If you turn back the pages of this book

Hint 1: If you're struggling, find someone who enjoys history.
Hint 2: There is a name that you know from recent pages.

Zero times do I lose a battle.
Each of my children is strong.
Under the world lives my brother.
Sometimes I use thunderbolts.

I am played by every land
Games where all come to play
The brightest, strongest stand
To get the gold to take away
Back to their proud land.

The next riddle, if solved, provides the answer to the first. But it spoils the previous three.

We were conquered by the Great
Told stories of the father of all Gods
Invented your Olympic Games
Have our own river Thames
But by our own country's name

The country Ilene is from is known for riddles and is known for the classic riddle of the sphinx. This riddle is found in the story of Oedipus.

A thing there is whose voice is one;
Whose feet are four and two and three.
So mutable a thing is none
That moves in earth or sky or sea.
When on most feet this thing doth go,
Its strength is weakest and its pace most slow.

Xaipete (Chairete) means *hello* in Greek. My name is Ilene, and I live in Athens, Greece. Riddles are a way of life for me. Greece is known for its great philosophers like Sophocles, Plato, and Aristotle. I am 9 years old. Most people's knowledge of Greece is all about ancient Greece. Modern-day Greece is beautiful as well. I love my life in Greece. I love to eat Moussaka. I also love to travel. However, I haven't been raised in only Greece. See if you can answer the following riddles to learn about where my father is from.

I am black and white but I don't say moo
I am kicked around but I don't say boo hoo
What am I?

Nice job solving these riddles! My father is from Rio, Brazil. Home to the Amazon Rainforest and known for being a land that loves to play soccer. The Amazon Rainforest is huge. 60% of the rainforest is found in Brazil. The Amazon Rainforest is one of my favorite topics. Some of the scariest, most wonderful creatures live in the Amazon Rainforest. Learning about the Amazon Rainforest is just one of my favorite things to do. See if you can solve the below riddles to learn about my favorite things.

Refer to the first letter
In order to find
Out what you don't know.
What is a city in Brazil?

130

A name you've heard me say
After the six before the seven
Like lasagna but in the Greek way
Lamb, tomatoes, and eggplant

131

I play on one that is Tall
But my favorite one is Old
Tall, Old, Yellow Socks
Describes the thing
I love to play with.

132

I'm what you do when you talk it out
After a fight, you've had with a friend
I also conceal areas you doubt
While enhancing what you intend
What am I?

133

I am when you put on an act
A lie you tell yourself to have fun
A role that is real or that is abstract
A game that doesn't require a ton
Maybe a simple sheet.
An innocent deceit
What am I playing?

134

Another word for being out of sight
Plus, another who discovers
is a game I love to play.
What game is it?

135

Known for success and prosperity
A leaf known symbolically
From it came the laureate
A modern-day version of the crown
Once worn by Greek and roman alike

136

What do all of these have in common?

Fingers, Nails, Hip, Bone, Blood, Muscle

137

My job requires patience
As I see a lot of patients
What am I?

138

I am the first layer hidden underneath
If left alone I'd turn into a pile of bones
The only part of me you see is my teeth
If you see other parts of me pick up the phone
Because you need a doctor to set it all straight
What am I?

139

A canopy of trees shrouds me in dark
Raindrops caught before they touch my ground
I am home to a fish scarier than a shark,
And a snake larger than any python you've found.
An amazing forest, I am?

✧ ✦ Chapter 5: Answers ✦

122. The man is from Greece while his partner is not. A sycophant in English is someone who flatters. While a sycophant in Greek is an informant. He bites a fig which is where the Greek word comes from. He only finds the joke funny because he is the only one that understands the different meanings of the same word.

123. Alexander the III, better known as Alexander the Great. His name is shared with 8-year-old Alex whom we got to learn about in previous chapters. Alexander the Great conquered all of Greece.

124. The first letter of each sentence fragment spells Zeus, who was the Greek ruler over all gods.

125. The Olympic games were invented in Ancient Greece. They promote peaceful competition where various countries compete to win gold medals.

126. Greece. England has a river Thames, but Greece also has a river named Thyamis.

127. Humans are born with one voice. We start out on 4 as babies. Learn to walk with two and in old age walk with a cane for three. Humans have learned to traverse water, earth, and sky. Lastly, humans' strength lies in their brains but it is a very weak body part too.

128. Soccer ball. Black and white but not a cow.

129. Rio is short for Brazil's capital Rio de Janeiro.

130. Moussaka, and it was mentioned before riddle 127 and after riddle 126.

131. Toys. Ilene loves to play with toys. The first letter of the capitalized words spells out Toys.

132. You can make up with a friend. And you can wear makeup.

133. Pretend play. Abstract means something you can't see, that doesn't take a physical form, like an idea. "Deceit" means a lie, but in this case, it is innocent because it's just for fun.

134. Hide-and-seek. Hide means be out of sight. Seek means to discover

135. Laurel wreaths were given to winner of competitions in ancient Greece and now that's why we call graduates laureates.

136. They have to do with the human body.

137. Doctor. Patience has two meanings: calmly waiting and someone a doctor helps

138. The skeleton. Teeth are part of our skeleton. If you see bones sticking out through someone's skin, you should pick up the phone and call for help because that person is hurt!

139. Amazon Rainforest. Piranhas are a scary fish found in the Amazon Rainforest, while anacondas are a large snake that also live there.

✳ *Chapter 6* ✳

Toys

Fantastic job! You've now learned a lot about me. You've learned about my love for toys, playing pretend, and hide-and-seek. You've also learned about laurels. Laurel wreaths began in ancient Greek culture. I like to weave together wreaths from our garden of laurel bushes. I also want to be a doctor when I grow up. I love learning about the human body. The muscles, skin, and skeletal system are incredible. Lastly, the Amazon Rainforest hails from my father's home and is super cool. In the next few chapters, you will dive into my life even further and learn about my love of toys, all about the body, and even the Amazon Rainforest.

✦ Chapter 6: *Toys* ✦

I love toys! See if you can guess the answers to these riddles that have everything to do with my favorite toys when I was a little kid and even some of my favorites now.

 140

If you build the tracks
We will race along all day
But make sure there are no cracks
Or we will fall down and lose our way
When we get to the finish line
You or your friends get to say hurray

141
You mold us with your hands
We can be one color or a rainbow
You make a face with hair strands
Or perhaps you make a ball grow
But make sure you put me away
Or else I'll crack and dry all day

142
I come with different shapes
But only one can fit one part
And babies can play me to learn
The shape of a square or heart

143
We can move from place to place
But only when your feet help
You all can use us to race
Use your balance and a helmet
Or you could fall upon your face

144
I am made of various clothes
To take you to various lands
As you pretend up various foes
You may store me in your closet
Or a basket, or even a chest
Unless you find I no longer fit

145
Ryan, Max, and Zelda bring various toys for a play date.
What is the favorite toy they bring?

Ryan brought	Balls
Max brought	Alphabet blocks
Zelda brought	Robots
Ryan brought	Barbies
Max brought	Insects
Zelda brought	Eeyore
Ryan brought	Slime

146

Kinetic or in a box or by the sea
We can come to you
When you cannot come to me
So, build castles at home or by the
Great big blue

147

The first part is something you do
when you're excited to get out of bed
The second part you find on a boat
As it aids you in hoisting and tying

148

I am in Raccoon but not Cocoon
I am in Oscar but not in Scar
I am in Boys but not in Yoyo's
I am in Son but not in Snail
I am in Tree but not in Respond
What am I?

149

I am known for helping a man make light
He tied a key to my string and put me up in the sky
He waited until a storm came by,

I am a _____

150

I am led by a conductor
I chug along some tracks
You may build my route

Or learn about _____ facts

151
I am a special kind of blocks
I teach you letter and sounds
You might say 's' is for socks
Or spill all of me on the ground

152
I am when you scratch your head
Or piece together a picture
If you're missing one of me
It might fill you up with dread
At the thought of never finishing me
What am I?

153
You throw me
You catch me
You run with me
You hit me
But hopefully you'll make it home
Without me
What am I?

154
You can make me like your house
With couches, beds, and all
The difference is that I am small
What am I?

155
You hit me to make music
But sometimes all you get is sound
You might find me therapeutic
As you play on my surface that is round

156 We can be almost anything
Cuddle sized to enormous
You might pretend we're marrying
We do whatever you inform us
We may protect you in your sleep
Or hold hands in the family jeep
What are we?

157 What unifies this toy?

✦ Chapter 6: Answers ✸

140. Hot Wheels or other forms of racing cars.

141. Play Doh, or some form of clay.

142. A shape sorter. A common toy is a lid with cut-out shapes, through which babies and toddlers try to fit the correct shape block.

143. Bikes or other transportation toys. Scooters, etc.

144. Dress up clothes. Dress up clothes are often stored all jumbled together in some kind of container.

145. Barbies. The first letter of the toys they bring spell BARBIES.

146. Sand. Kinetic sand is a kind of sand that sticks together. It also comes in a box or from the beach, so you can use it even if you're not by the ocean.

147. Jump rope. You want to jump out of bed. And you use rope to tie things and hoist things on a boat.

148. Robot is spelled when you find the unique letter.

149. Kite. Thomas Jefferson used a key tied to a kite to do experiments with lightning that led to discoveries about electricity.

150. Train. A train conductor is someone who makes sure the train runs safely. A common toy for kids is train tracks that they can build themselves.

151. Alphabet blocks.

152. Puzzle. Have you ever lost the last piece of a puzzle? Oh no!

153. Baseball. When you hit a baseball in a game, you want to hit it far enough so that you have enough time to make it to the home base.

154. Dollhouse.

155. Drum. Sometimes it's therapeutic (calming) to hit a drum!

156. Stuffed animals. These are great toys for imaginative (pretend) play.

157. The toy is made out of multiple toys but specifically all toys that start with the letter "B".

Chapter 7

Human Body

Nice job learning about all the toys that I grew up with. Next, you'll learn all about what I spend most of my free time learning. Because I am going to be a doctor! This means I need to know all I can about the human body.

158

What can you hear but never see
The first thing that a baby can control
But something that you can't touch
What am I?

159

I am a system fueled by the _____
If I am gone it all falls apart
The first of my kind from the start

160

I have 12 heads with faces
I have 13 hearts with no organs
Even though I have no arms and legs,
I can still club you.
What am I?

161

I am an organ that you can see
I help you to speak
What am I?

162. When you are sick, I come to your aid
I am in blood but I am not red
I am a cell but not locked in a cage
What am I?

163. If you spend too long in the pool
You will find that I become present
In your hands, sometimes feet too
You'll think you've suddenly aged
But I'm really just a short-term tool

164. I am ATGC or is it CTGA
I am a book in the body
Written in code that
Holds a lot of sway

165. I am a useful part of the body
But am often overlooked
Think of me like a filter
As you take in what is cooked

166. There are two of me
If there were none
You'd have to use your mouth
I am perhaps the most important
As you use me every day
But you could try to tie me up
Though you'd also tie up my friend
And you'll soon find that my friends
Help you to not fall down
But I'll ease your ability to get up

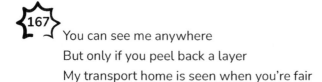
You can see me anywhere
But only if you peel back a layer
My transport home is seen when you're fair

I am another name for a student of a teacher
Or I can be something that changes in a different light
I am a?

A baseball _____
Is part two of me
The first you will find
Rhymes with tree

What do these words have in common?

Hear, China, Farm, Clip, Hearth

171
I am a shade of pink
I am your body's response
When the heart causes me to appear

I begin to race
As you make your way uphill
If you start a chase
Then it's me you may start to feel

I am only useful with light
I am one of the weakest parts,
But because of my strengths
We can even see the stars.

We have the biggest of any species
It's why our babies have such a big head
You've used it to solve these riddles
In order to use it you have to go to bed

When liquid splashes me,
none seeps through, when I'm moved a lot
Liquid I spew, When I am hit, color I change,
And I come in quite a range, what I cover
is quite complex, yet I am very easy to flex.
What am I?

Even though we live different lives
we are all so very similar, we grow old
At the end of it all, the infinite archives
We realize that all of us is made up of _____

What is the similarity of every figure in the image?

158. The voice can be heard but not seen. The only thing a baby can control at first is their cry. You cannot touch your voice.

159. The heart fuels the organs in the body with blood. The heart is the first-formed organ in the mother's womb.

160. A deck of cards. A deck has 12 face cards. The King, Queen, and Jack all have faces and there are 4 suits. 1 suit is hearts and there are 13 cards in each suit.

161. The tongue is a muscular organ.

162. The white blood cell protects us from illness and fights bacteria and viruses.

163. The wrinkles in our hands and feet after spending time in water create grooves in our skin that allow us to have a better grip on slippery surfaces.

164. DNA makes up the coding of our bodies. It can determine our likelihood of having certain diseases in our lives or whether we have blonde hair or brown eyes.

165. The nose. The nose is located just below the eyes, so it is often 'overlooked'. The nose helps us filter air but also filters what food we eat by its smell.

166. The hand. Perhaps the most useful body part we have. It's attached to the arms which helps us to maintain our balance as we walk. If we fall our hands help us to get a grip so we can more easily stand back up.

167. Blood. Blood can be seen if you cut any part of the body. Veins carry blood back to the heart like a transportation service.

168. Pupil. A pupil is a student. A pupil is also found in the eye and changes size depending on how much light the eye is taking in.

169. A kneecap. Cap is the second part of the word. And knee rhymes with tree.

170. They are all parts of the body if you take away one letter. Chin, arm, heart, lip, ear.

171. Blush. Blush depending on the individual is a shade of pink. When our heart pumps more oxygen into our cheeks we blush.

172. The heart races as you begin to work your muscles. If you work them hard enough you can even feel your heart beating in your chest.

173. The eyes. The eyes are only useful with light. But even the tiniest amount of light lets us see. This is why even when it is completely dark, we can still see stars at night.

174. The brain. Sleep helps your brain to function.

175. Skin. The skin protects from liquids. You sweat when you exert yourself. If you get hit hard you bleed red. Humans, come in all different shades. And skin covers our complex system of bones, muscles, and tissues.

176. Code. Humans as they have evolved have had DNA code, all the way to the digital UPC line (or barcode), which is also made up of codes.

Chapter 8

The Amazon Rainforest

I hope you loved learning about the body as much as I did! Now we can turn our attention to one of the scariest yet most beautiful places on Earth. Filled with scary creatures that almost seem unreal. My father has taken me to the Amazon Rainforest nearby his hometown. When I enter the rainforest, it feels like I am entering an entirely new world! See if you can solve these riddles about the rainforest.

177

I am the largest eagle of all
the closest to my raptor relatives
The other half of my name
Is also found in Greek mythology
What am I?

178

My first of the second word is the tears cried by clouds
The second a large area covered in trees
But before that name appears another
Also found in Greek mythology
Women known for their height and strength
Who trained a woman of wonder
Found in your TV.

179

I have no color
I have no odor
I have no taste
The Amazon creates me
And you consume me
What am I?

One friend is the largest and covers most land
The second salty and confined
I often run to my first friend
My third friend is where I sometimes start
They are also mostly confined.
But we are all the same mostly
Except I get to roam the countryside

I am sometimes a cloth covering something
Or I am known to be actively doing something
I protect the ground from the hot rays of the sun
I start with a c
Though when I end you may say why?

I am called a gold lion
But I do not venture on the ground
You'll find me in the canopy
I make a bird-like sound
Though I am not a bird.

My first part is known as always, or at any time
My second is like Christmas except not red, I'm _____
You put both of me together
I become a tree, what am I?

When I am hot you feel sticky
When I am cold you feel you cannot ever get warm
But when my brother is hot you feel dry
And when he is cold you can bundle up
What am I?

I am called this when I create growth year-round

I am called this when the land I'm in never frosts

I am called this when I maintain moisture in the air

If you take away one letter to me you get topical.

 I am grown in the canopy shade

Though I take a long time to fruit

I quickly help your parents to get paid

Known for my dark brown color

I'm in shops across the world

But I can even be homemade

 I am so important as I am a home

To half the animals and plants

Even some that roam

Protect me if you can.

 I walk on two legs but it's not how I'm known to move

I build my own home but I have no arms

I travel across continents but don't use a boat.

What am I?

 I am the original green army

In the forest, we number in the 1000s

If your eyes were like mine

They'd sit atop your forehead

What am I?

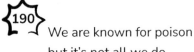

190
We are known for poison
but it's not all we do
I wrap myself around my prey
In one bite I eat my food.

191
When you cut me down the middle
You'll find you need to fiddle
To get through all the way
Because once you have me open
You'll find my center hardly broken
Spread me on toast
Add me to a smoothie
You'll find I'm quite tasty

192
Peel and then split
Then do it twice
You'll have something nice
To enjoy with a friend
on a nice hot day

193
I am the strongest cat
I have the strongest bite
I swim when other cats are not a fan
My spots have spots
What am I?

The man walked away with not even a scar.
What killed the man?

177. The Harpy Eagle is known as the jaguar of the sky in the Amazon Rainforest. The harpy in Greek mythology was a frightening predator. Half woman half bird.

178. The Amazon Rainforest. The name Amazon comes from the Amazon River but its name comes from Greek mythology, namely the Amazonian women warriors. Wonder Woman was raised by the Amazon women.

179. Air. More specifically, Oxygen. 20% of the world's oxygen is created by the Amazon Rainforest.

180. A river. The largest friend is the ocean, the second is a sea. The third is a lake which can sometimes start a river as it then roams the land and often finds itself running into an ocean or sometimes another lake. The Amazon is home to the largest river, the Amazon River.

181. Canopy. Starts with a c and ends with a y. The Amazon Rainforest is known for its canopy, which stops the rain from falling to the ground for an estimated 10 minutes.

182. The Gold Lion Tamarin is a monkey that makes a shrieking sound almost like a bird.

183. Evergreen tree. Christmas colors are red and green. The word ever can be used to mean always or at any time. The evergreen tree makes up the rainforest.

184. Humidity. Humid air is moist and makes you sticky, and makes it harder to warm up since you are wet. Humidity's brother is dry air. The rainforest is humid.

185. Tropical. When you add the r.

186. Coffee. Coffee is grown in rainforests.

187. The rainforest is home to many animals and plant life. Many animals must travel to tropical areas to escape the harsh winter of their native lands.

188. A bird. The Amazon Rainforest is home to the largest variety of bird species.

189. A frog. The Amazon Rainforest is home to over 1,000 different frog species.

190. Snake. The Amazon Rainforest is home to the largest snake, the green anaconda.

191. Avocado. An avocado is only one of many fruits produced in the rainforest.

192. A banana split. Bananas are also mainly produced in the rainforests.

193. The Jaguar. A native cat to the Amazon Rainforest. It has the strongest bite of all of the large cats.

194. A mosquito. One of the deadliest things in the Amazon Rainforest is the pathogen-carrying mosquitos. All the information provided is that the man walked away but we do see them being bit by a mosquito. Luckily, we have many preventative measures we can take such as vaccinations to keep us safe from mosquitos in the Amazon.

Chapter 9

Meet Zackary

✦✦ *Chapter 9:* *Meet Zackary* ✦✦

> Before we meet Zackary, we will need to learn a bit about somewhere he doesn't live before we learn about where he does live. Zackary is tricky. He won't let you figure out where he is from without lots of effort. So, he has numerous riddles leading to the answers you're searching for. Someone with knowledge of both science and history may be able to help out with 196 and 197.

195
I am my own land
Sometimes those lost at sea
Land upon my shores
A time of old left us isolated
Standing firm against the waves
Dangerous storms come
Where am I?

196
You may have heard the prior clue
To which of us that are famous, I'll tell you
A place that set the stage for our rat race
Filled with birds, I set a galloping pace
A novel idea of evolution transfixed our land
Into a source of contention both old and new
And now science and religion often feud

197
We make our way through history
As we find the island's most famous
One of which remains a mystery
Our friend Ilene likely can name us
A city often described in fable and myth
Seen from stories of the little mermaid
An ocean that continues to be surveyed.

The previous two riddles told us about various famous places that all have to do with a common theme. Keep that in mind as we use the next two clues to discover a word we will need to figure out where Zackary is from.

{198}
I am found in nature
You can find me in your foot
You can find me built in Paris
I represent triumph
As I support buildings, empires
And even your body.

{199}
I am by myself
When I am big - I stand alone
When I am small a small dot
gives me company overhead
I am often crowded by others.
I see six standing tall
While four shelter under a dot.

{200}
I am not used today to mean
What I used to mean
Now only a village is named after me
At one time I had been the name for sea
If you take one hundred and ninety-seven
And one hundred and ninety-eight
Add that to me and you get a vocab lesson
A group of islands after you translate

If you've been finding the answers, we now have two helpful hints in figuring out where Zachary is from. The first is some sort of island. The second is more specifically an archipelago. Zachary is from a group of islands. Now let's try to get closer to where this group of islands may be.

201
I am land to the tallest
I am the second biggest
I am land to the largest
Once home to the richest
I am known as the hottest
I am the mother of all

202
You probably came here for a safari
But then you learned more about me
A Jane that studied chimpanzees
A rocker who you may know as Queen

203
If you travel southwest from 201
You'll find me sitting there
For a time, the rest of the world had none
With ring-like tails, a blue-eyed stare,
Many endangered efforts have begun
Now you can find us everywhere

204
I lay west of 202 though only a small spot you'll find
Here you will see Zackary trying to unwind
A land colonized by the Dutch as they explore
Australia. Then the French took over but more,
For aiding their naval fleet. then the Isle de France
Until their defeat.

Bonzur! That is how you say *hello* in Mauritian Creole. I am Zachary, but you can call me Zack. I live in the small archipelago of Mauritius. I love island life. Our home is a tourist spot much like Hawaii. I have met many different kinds of people growing up here. Our home is a melting pot of people, but we are primarily of Indo-Pakistani descent. Both of my parents hail from Mauritius and we have a long history here that dates back to the 1600s. I am 10 years old and I have learned three different languages. See if you can solve the below riddles to get clues about which languages I speak.

205 Find what is unique about this sentence

> *The quick brown fox jumps over the lazy dog*

206 When I say eighty, you say four twenties
Though I say ninety-nine you say
Four twenties, ten, nine
Though you say that you are most beautiful
Your counting is quite Gaelic

207 I am created from dissonance
As two groups merge into one
One group who seek deliverance
As two languages come undone
You find a clue in Zack's first word
As you see something similar
Completely changed.
Completely new.

Yes, great job. I speak three different languages. This helps me to interact with most people who come to visit. I would love for you to learn more about some of my favorite things to do and learn.

208

A subject that always grows
It never remains the same
It even changes when placed
In someone else's hands.
We are told to learn from it
So, we don't repeat past mistakes

You've learned my three favorite things to study about. I absolutely love sports, all kinds of sports. I am constantly asking tourists about their favorite sports. I also love history. There is a rich history in the whole world but nowhere is it richer than in Africa. The place where we all once originated. Lastly, the most fascinating thing to me about Africa is the Sahara Desert. Nomads still to this day travel across the Saharan desert in search of water and food. The last two riddles have to do with my favorite foods. See if you can guess them.

209

Don't begin your trek
Unless you're fully prepared
The harshest climate you'll face
With tortuous days and freezing nights
Only a few plants and animals live
In such a place

210

I hail from India
You can order me mild
Medium or spicy
I can be yellow, green, brown
And even red
But I will keep you well fed

211

I look like fish eggs on the inside but I am not fish eggs
I will dye your table cloth red but I am not blood
I have juice that bursts into your mouth but I'm not a gusher
The edible fruit inside is as small as a kernel but I'm not popcorn
What am I?

212

I've existed for thousands of years
Originally a way to better train
For the hunt as we hurled spears
Now a form of competition to attain
Great respect from all your peers

✦ *Chapter 9: Answers* ✦

195. On an Island. As it spells and describes the island.

196. Darwin's Island, which was in the Galapagos Islands. His research led to our modern understanding of the evolution of species as well as our own.

197. The City of Atlantis. Ilene, one of our friends in this book, loves aquatic life, so she probably knows about the City of Atlantis.

198. An Arch. We have four arches in our foot. One famous monument in France is the Arc de Triumph.

199. An "I" or an "i." There are six uppercase I's and four lowercase i's.

200. Pelago. Is the ancient Greek word for sea. If you looked up what a group of islands are called—you would find the archipelago. This is where you take the answer of 197 then 198 and add them together to find the full word. Taking it apart gives you the answer.

201. The continent of Africa is home to the largest and tallest land animals. It is the second biggest continent. It is home to history's wealthiest ruler - Mansa Musa. It is on the equator and is home to the hottest desert in the world. Africa is known as the mother continent as all humans hail from Africa.

202. Tanzania is where Jane Goodall studied chimps. It is also where Freddie Mercury was born.

203. The lemur. Lemurs are only home to Madagascar. Until efforts to repopulate them led them to many other lands.

204. Mauritius Island. Zackary lives on the island of Mauritius.

205. The sentence contains each letter of the English alphabet.

206. French. French is a romance language. But its counting system mimics those of Gaelic languages.

207. Creole. Creole typically happens in places where a dominating language attempted to take over. As individuals continued to speak their original language while still learning some of the new, a new combined language was born. There are many examples of Creole languages, such as Jamaican Creole. In Zack's case, Mauritian Creole.

208. History. History always grows and changes because it is ongoing and depends on events that take place. It can change in someone else's hands because they will tell it from their point of view. A common saying is that we must learn from history so that we don't repeat it.

209. The desert. To travel in the desert, you must plan carefully as there is little there to help with your survival.

210. Curry. Curry originates from India and comes in different strengths and colors.

211. A pomegranate. It looks like a fish egg and has a red color that can stain.

212. Sports. Many sports originate from physical skills used to help humans hunt for food. Great athletes are respected by their teammates and opponents.

Chapter 10

Sports

✦✦ *Chapter 10: Sports* ✦✦

> **I love playing all sorts of sports. See if you can solve these riddles all about sports!**

{213}
I travel faster when I am thrown
than I do when I am hit
Unless I am taken home

{214}
A sport requiring technique
too fast to understand
though invented in England
China has taken titles and run
A sport perfect for any age

{215}
The strongest athletes in the world
make up those that play this sport
but because they swirl and twirl
more females show up in the report

{216}
A sport dominated by the tall.
Someone shorter would need to find
a way to get around the tall wall.
To take advantage of the ball.

217
Your goal is to serve
You want to hold that spot
You work your way up to it
All the while making sure
To not let it double drop
in your spot.

218
A rope and a ball
If I clock it clockwise
Then I'll have won
If they counter
Until the rope is gone
Then they'll have won

219
I have the biggest field but I'm not football
I play with a HORSE but I'm not basketball
I play with a stick but I'm not hockey
What am I?

220
I wrestle but in boots
my opponent is a man
but I do not wrestle him
instead, we compete
over the time that it takes
to steer to the ground

I show the most skin,
but I don't go in water
I am the heaviest I can be,
but I am still agile.
My feet must stay firm
For being an unmovable
rock cuts my life long term

 I am a transport that has no wheels
I ride through tunnels that I can touch
My direction adjusted through the heels
As you shred through you feel a rush

 Find the commonality

Sam shoots baskets, Lexy kicks goals, Travis serves with
backspin, Stacey does jump serves

 You jump hundreds of times but it's not jumping rope.
Being tall is advantageous but it's not basketball.
You use rally point scoring but it's not badminton
What am I?

225 A single game of me can last many days
I am more popular than baseball worldwide
If you are from America, you likely referred to me
As Pinocchio's little friend.

226 I hailed from the maple leaf
With a puck and a stick
Which is quite a relief
Since I used to use
frozen cow dung

227 I need someone to carry my bag
the tools I have are many
when I have fewer points, I brag

228 Only one can hold me with their hands
though they only have six seconds to decide
Head points make for an eruption in the stands
I am a source of many countries' pride

229 What runs around the football field but never moves?

Which game shows a point being scored?

213. Baseball. A baseball travels faster when it is thrown than when it is hit, but if it's hit hard enough, it can help you run to home base.

214. Ping pong. It's a speedy game that kids can play. China dominates at elite ping pong!

215. Gymnastics. Gymnasts are extremely strong as well as showing creative flair.

216. Basketball. Most basketballers are very tall, but shorter players also have important roles in the game due to their ball skills and positioning.

217. Four square. Each player stands in one of four squares. The aim is to make your way to the King square, where the player who starts the game by serving stands. Every time you win, you move up a square. You can't let the ball bounce twice in your square or you're out!

218. Tetherball. The ball is hit (or "clocked") around the pole. When you have hit the ball around the pole in your direction (in this case, clockwise) and there is no rope left, you have won!

219. Polo. Polo is played on a large field. HORSE is a common basketball drill. Polo players use a stick to hit the ball while riding on a horse.

220. Steer wrestling. This is a rodeo event in which a horse-mounted rider chases a steer, jumps on it, and then wrestles the steer to the ground. Riders dress like cowboys and wear boots. They try to "drop" their steer faster than their opponents.

221. Sumo Wrestling. Sumo wrestlers live considerably less time due to the strain they put on their bodies.

222. Surfboard. Surfers steer their board through tunnels made from waves, known as a "barrel". Surfers sometimes touch the wave with their hand to keep their balance, while steering with their feet. A good surfer "shreds" and doing so spikes your adrenaline (giving you a rush!).

223. They all play sports with balls.

224. Volleyball. Volleyball involves lots of jumping to direct the ball over the net. Players are often tall, and the scoring system is similar to that of other net sports like badminton.

225. Cricket. A game of cricket that is a "test match" can last several days. Cricket is played mainly by Commonwealth countries with ties with the United Kingdom. Americans don't typically play cricket and think of "cricket" as referring to the wooden boy's friend in the children's story and movie, Pinocchio.

226. Ice Hockey. The game originates from Canada, which is represented by a maple leaf. At first, for a puck, players used to use frozen cow dung! Gross!

227. Golf. Golf players have someone carry their bag of golf clubs (tools), called a "caddy." Unlike most sports, the winner in golf has the least number of points.

228. Soccer. Only the goalkeeper can touch the ball with their hands, but they have to throw it in six seconds. When a player uses their head to direct the ball into the goals, it's very exciting. Soccer (or "football") is a very popular game in many countries.

229. A fence. Here the word "runs" means "extend in a particular direction," rather than the act of running using your legs.

230. The volleyball hitting the floor is the only demonstrated point being scored in these three pictures.

Chapter 11

History

✦✦ *Chapter 11: History* ✦✦

> I love history and learning about all the different countries in the world!

231

I am portrayed with wooden teeth
but I'm more known for my humility
I crossed the river of the Delaware
In search of my own sense of civility
I stepped down from the power
An unprecedented move of gentility

232

The first says that I am free
The second says I can defend
The third protects me from government
The fourth lends me privacy
The fifth ensures I receive due process

233

If you count the number of wars
That has existed throughout time
You'd find that there would be more of me
I'm a type of treat but you'll find me not so sweet
As you see me throughout years of diplomacy

234

What is the commonality to these words

Golden, Bronze, Middle, Dark, Iron

235

I allowed the growth of culture
Because I increased the growth of food
Cities exist because of me
Luxuries exist because of me
Because there was a time where all humanity
Hunted and gathered for food
But now that I exist those efforts worldwide subdued.

 236

The first part of me is not a girl but a _____
The second part, a baby's bed or camp bed
When you bring the two words together
It's a form of rebellion of an organization

 237

If I say I give you this
You say you give me that
But we never trade with dollar bills
Instead, we say a donkey for a cat

 238

You may be making a fuss
If you find someone being sus
But unless a jury loses trust
Then you might be stuck at a loss
Because we all have the right to a

Fair _____

The next number of riddles are all about inventions that
changed history forever.

{239} I changed the world through words
as thousands more came into being
no longer by hand but now in mass
all due to the invention of this press

{240} For a long time, we looked at a star
Then I came along, controlled by the pull
Of the earth, you now could travel far
Knowing your direction
At any given time.

{241} When I came about you could talk
without talking, I travel far so you
don't have to, with words without lips
spoken as you unravel me to read

{242} I replaced the campfire and candle
now you can wake up when you sleep
and walk into the bathroom
with a simple switch of the _____

{243} I am a form of transport
an aid to the hunt
a weapon in war
as we storm speedily to the front

{244} I took over 241
which was enhanced by 239
Now you see me at 244
And you're using 2 or 1 of those
But you probably don't go a day
without me

245
The thought of me seemed
a distant dream you'd never
believe. The thought of being
a bird to travel over the sea

246
I am round in shape
made to roll down and up
the invention of me
made your stuff less stuck

247
For almost 200 years I settled discontent
For over 200 years I've thrived alive and free
All the while I survived and won WW I and II
It all started when I threw out England's tea.

248

What is in seasons, seconds, centuries, and minutes,
but not in decades, years, or days?

231. George Washington. He was rumored to have wooden teeth as is famous for being a caring leader. During the American Revolutionary War, Washington led troops across the Delaware River. He was the United States' first president. When he decided to retire, he laid the foundation for America's democratic system of government, by giving up power willingly and allowing it to pass peacefully to the next elected leader.

232. The first five amendments of the Constitution.

233. A treaty. There are more treaties than there are wars. More efforts toward peace than fighting.

234. The words refer to different ages in history. The Middle Ages are also known as the dark ages.

235. Agriculture. Agriculture helped humans grow stronger and smarter, leading culture to thrive. Cities came to be as hubs where food from across a region could be bought and sold. Originally, the only way humans could get food was by hunting and gathering. Agriculture allowed humans to stay put in one place and grow or breed their food. This led to better and better ways of living, as well as to transport food around the world.

236. Boycott. Not a girl = a boy. A baby's bed or a camp bed = cot. When people want to make a point to an organization, to rebel against it, they "boycott" it. This means they don't buy from that organization or use its services, in the hope of changing their behavior.

237. Bartering. When people trade items instead of money, they are bartering.

238. Trial. A trial involves a jury making a decision about a person's guilt or innocence. Even though we might think someone is guilty, a fair trial is needed to make an unbiased decision. Everyone has a right to defend their innocence.

239. Printing press. When the printing press was invented, it changed the world forever, as now people could share their ideas on a much wider scale and much more easily.

240. The compass. People used to use the stars to navigate. The compass uses magnetism (the pull of the earth) to show you the direction of north. Therefore, it helps people to get around without relying on a clear night's sky.

241. Paper. Paper allowed people to communicate without speaking and send news and information all over by using the mail. Letters were written on paper and sent in envelopes or tied up in scrolls, each of which needed to be unraveled to read them.

242. The light bulb. Before the lightbulb, humans used fire for light. Now, even when it's dark at night, we can easily see because of electricity.

243. Horse. When horses were tamed (domesticated), they were able to be used for transport, for hunting, and for fighting in wars.

244. The internet.

245. Airplane. Before they were invented, airplanes were hard to imagine. We could look at birds and see them fly, but it was hard to believe that humans would ever take flight!

246. Wheel. Before the wheel, it was much harder for humans to transport things.

247. United States of America was settled from 1604-1776, an independent nation from 1776 to the present. Winners of WWI and II and they threw England's tea in the Boston River.

248. The letter N. It is the only letter that you can't find in the words mentioned in the riddle.

Chapter 12

Deserts

✦✦ Chapter 12: Deserts ✦✦

{249}

One thing to understand about deserts
Is that they are like a Katie Perry song
During the day they are this
During the night they are that
But some deserts are known for this
While deserts like the tundra are known for that
What is this? What is that?

{250}

I am an action that is taken
To survive the desert heat
If I bury myself below
I might get some relief

{251}

I am a large hill difficult to climb
Endless mountains and hills
A sea of sand is found
If you make it to my top
You can peer down
All you'll find is sand

{252}

I have one hump
Sometimes i have two
If you sit atop
You might get to
Where you need
To go

{253}

I am green but live among little rain
I am spiky but can give life's water
To those critters caught with pain
Of thirst who need it quenched

{254} I am ice cold in a desert
That you may not know
One that is frozen solid
Filled with fresh water
As i melt it causes change

{255} I am in the thousands
The hundreds of thousands
I can dance i can sway
I can bury i can flee
You find me here
But you also find me there

{256} If you have me
You may not last much longer
I am what happens
When you don't drink enough water

{257} If you are poisoned by me
You may not last very long
There are so many of me
In the desert you'd better
Take your time

{258} I am a gust of wind
A storm that has no rain
If you get caught
You may get buried

So many imagine i exist
As they cross the desert plain
Sometimes i am real
Sometimes you sure in vain
If you find me though
You won't have need of rain

 If you do not protect yourself
You may go insane
Because the land of the desert
Has nearly no rain
So, you must have me
You need to cover up
In order to protect yourself
From the sun

 I am a burning star in the sky
But you don't know me as a star
If i was gone you wouldn't be here
But if you're too close to me
You will also die

A camel driver has to cross the desert and get to the Nile River to transport his merchandise. It takes six weeks to cross the desert and get to the Nile River. He can only carry four weeks of food for himself and his camel at any time because the camel also has to carry his merchandise. If he cannot get help from anyone else or get any more camels, and there is an unlimited supply of food where he is, how can he cross the desert and get to the Nile River?

Four men walk into the desert. Suddenly all four are simultaneously knocked out. They awake buried to their heads in the sand unable to look anywhere but straight ahead. They are positioned so that each man sees another's head before him. However, between the first and second man, there is a separating wall. So, the first man sees only the desert. The second man sees only the wall. The third man sees another's head and a wall. The fourth man sees two heads and a wall. On top of each man's head is a hat. The underside of each cap is black, but the outside of each cap is either blue or white. Before any of the men can speak, their captors tell them if they speak, they die. However, if any of them can guess the color of their cap on the first try they go free. The captors tell them that there are two blue caps and two white caps. Being an omniscient observer of the situation, we know that the order of the caps is: blue, white, blue, white. So, knowing the perspective of each man in the sand, and that they can only see the color of caps/wall/desert in front of them, which of the four men knows for certain the color of his own cap. More importantly: why?

 I am a description that you give an animal
That only travels around at night
If you see me my eyes likely glow
A fiery white or gold as i take in the moonlight

249. Hot and cold. Katy Perry's song is called "Hot and Cold." During the day, desserts are hot but at night, they are cold. Some desserts are known for being hot while others are known for being cold.

250. Burrow. Animals burrow into the ground or sand to survive in the dessert when it's hot. Under the surface, it's much cooler.

251. Sand dune. It's hard to climb a hill made of sand. From the top of a sand dune, as far as the eye can see is more sand.

252. Camel. Camels have one or two humps and are used for transport in the desert.

253. Cactus. These plants can survive with little water. In the desert, insects go to cacti to find water.

254. Glacier. Glaciers are found in environments that are like frozen deserts. They are filled with fresh water. The world's glaciers are melting due to changes in the climate.

255. Sand. Sand is made of many, many grains. It can blow in the wind, bury things, and suddenly disappear, moving from here to there very quickly.

256. Dehydration. This is a serious condition caused by not drinking enough water.

257. Snake. Snake bites can poison you, sometimes with serious consequences. Snakes are found in many desert environments, so if you're in one, you should keep an eye out!

258. Sandstorm. It has no rain because the storm is of sand not water. A sandstorm can cause a lot of sand to build up in one place, maybe burying anyone stuck there.

259. Oasis. There is little rain in the dessert, which makes it hard for humans to survive there without care. An oasis is a place in the dessert where water is found—a welcome relief! Sometimes, people traveling in the desert imagine that there is an oasis nearby.

260. Head covering. Keeping your head covered in the desert is important because of the extreme heat and the sun's harsh rays.

261. Sun. Yes, the sun is actually a star! Planet Earth needs the sun to survive. However, if you got too close to the sun, you'd burn up quick.

262. He takes four weeks of food and leaves two weeks of food supplies in the one-week mark and goes back with the one week of food supply left. Then he goes back with four weeks of food and picks up one week of food supplies from the one-week mark giving him four again in total. He leaves two weeks of supply in the two-week mark and goes back to the one-week mark and picks up the one-week food supply to go back. Then he leaves with the four weeks of food supply and goes to the two-week mark and picks up the two-week food supplies that were there, giving him four weeks of food again, then he goes to the Nile River with the four weeks of food supplies.

263. The third man. This is because he knows there are only two of each color cap. If the man behind him (the fourth man) saw two caps that were the same color in front of him, he would know that his own must be the opposite. However, because the caps alternate in color, the fourth man has only a 50% chance of getting his hat color correct, so therefore he stays quiet. The third man realizes that the fourth man is quiet because he cannot not see two caps of the same color in front of him, otherwise the fourth man would say the opposite of the caps in front of him. Therefore, the third man presumes his own cap must be the opposite of the man in front of him, and his presumption is correct. Under this same logic, after the third man speaks his color hat, the second man, even though he sees only wall, would be the next to go free, because he knows his cap must be the opposite of whichever color the third man's cap was.

264. Nocturnal. Lots of nocturnal animals have eyes that glow in the dark.

Chapter 13

Meet Jonelle

Chapter 13: Meet Jonelle

Before we have a chance to meet Jonelle, we need to solve the riddles below in order to figure out where Jonelle is from.

265
An original 13
I am such a peach
Making fried chicken
And heading south to
The beach

If you don't know it yet look through the next riddles for more clues.

266
I am a monkey
As curious as can be
You find my name on tv
If you know it
It holds a key
To a riddle about
One of thirteen

267
I am first part cow and second part common human support animal.
What am I?

268
Maybe
Look
Karefully to find a famous man

269
The first part is the opposite of sour
The second was spilt in the Boston Harbor

I'm cute tiny characters on your screen
or perhaps I'm at a gallery
or even still maybe you'll find
you eat me at a circus to pass the time

Howdy! My name is Jonelle and I'm from Macon, Georgia. I'm twelve years old and I absolutely love living in Georgia. If you solved the above riddles, then you would start to understand that Georgia is famous for a lot of things. We've got the Georgia Bulldogs football team. We're home to sweet tea and where Martin Luther King was born. And we produce the most amounts of peanuts in all of the United States of America. Next, see if you can solve these few riddles to learn about things I love!

 The first part is another name for soda
The second is more complicated
Take a snapshot of all my friends you've
Learned about in Chapters 1, 5, 9, and 13

And you take a snapshot of their _____

 If I take my creativity and I splatter it here
If i take my imagination and paint it there
If i mold my thoughts and feelings freely
Then perhaps i will make something
That will outlive me
What have i made?

 If I look up to the sky
And then try to look farther
What do i see?

274

If I stop, drop, and roll
If you watch me whip
I'll watch you nae nae
But if you can't do the floss
I assume you'd be lost
What am I doing?

275

First part an older term
For old english
Second part a device
That gives you access to all knowledge
In the palm of your hand
You bring these two together
You create soulful music

276

If you got Georgia on your Mind
Then Say a little prayer
Because It's a Man's World
And you can't be no Pushover
So Please, Please, Please
Have a little Respect

For my _____

277

Awe, you're such a peach
He says to me
As i watch him gobble

Up his peach _____

You've learned about my love of dancing, soul music, and peach cobbler. But now get to know some of the people that I most look up to.

278
I am the 49th
But i am 3x the 1st
This nation has ever seen
When it looks into the screen
An unprecedented second
For a woman mixed between

279
I am referred to as a queen
But i am not royalty
Known as a Grammy machine
My music is high quality

280
My sister and i both play tennis
Both better than 99%, we shine
You've only heard of me, in fairness
I have 73 titles while she has 49

281
I have spent over two decades
On the tv, but haven't been
For the past 10. Yet you have
Still probably heard of me
A billionaire and a woman
Who's known for being on TV

I've been to the Olympics,
Gymnastics is my sport.
I have earned more medals
Than any other gymnast in the world

Now that you have learned more about my idols, you can solve the next number of riddles in these upcoming chapters to learn more about the subjects I love.

✧ *Chapter 13: Answers* ✶

265. Georgia. Georgia is one of the original 13 colonies of the United States of America. It is one of the top peach-producing states and is also known for its fried chicken. If you travel south of Georgia, you'll find the beach.

266. Curious George. This is a children's TV character who is a monkey. "George" is similar to "Georgia".

267. Bull dogs. A bull is an adult male cow. Dogs are known for being a great support to humans.

268. Martin Luther King. The start of each word forms the initials "MLK." Martin Luther King Jr., the most well-known civil rights activist, was often known by his initials.

269. Sweet tea. The opposite of sour is sweet. Famously, in the lead up to the American Revolutionary War, opponents to British rule of America tipped tea into the Boston Harbor as a protest against taxation.

270. Peanuts. Peanuts is a popular comic strip that features tiny characters. The "peanut gallery" is a phrase referring to the cheap seats in a theater. Peanuts are a common snack enjoyed at the circus.

271. Pop culture. In some places soda is called "pop." All the friends described in the book have a culture.

272. Art. Art involves creativity, imagination and making something to express our ideas. Art will outlive you, even after you're gone.

273. Outer space. Beyond the sky is outer space.

274. Dancing. The clues in the riddle all refer to different dancing styles and trends.

275. Saxophone. "Saxon" is an older term for old English. A phone can be used to find out information and can be held in your hand. Sax + phone = saxophone.

276. Soul. The clues in the riddle are all song titles and lyrics associated with Soul music. A soul is also the name of the spiritual part of humans that represent our selves.

277. Peach cobbler. This is a popular dish in Georgia.

278. Kamala Harris. Harris was the 49th Vice President of the United States. She also achieved three (3x) other firsts: first female vice president, first African American vice president, and first Asian American vice president. Previously, she became the second African American woman to serve in the United States Senate.

279. Beyonce. Often nicknamed "Queen," Beyonce has won many Grammy Awards for her music.

280. Serena Williams. Williams has a twin sister named Venus who is also a tennis player. Both sisters are very successful in their sport, though Serena has achieved more titles.

281. Oprah Winfrey. Winfrey's TV show, Oprah, ran from 1985 to 2011.

282. Simone Biles. Biles is the world's best gymnast.

Chapter 14

Pop Culture

✦✦ Chapter 14: Pop Culture ✦✦

> One of my favorite past times is enjoying the latest trends in entertainment. See if you can solve the below riddles all about some of my generation's favorite things.

{283} I move left to right, forward and back,
I can clean. I can dance. What am I doing?

{284} I am a super-hero that transcends time
But you are more likely to know the multiverse
Because you've watched my timeline
Though i don't fly i can move almost as fast
As i jump through the air what is it that i have to catch?

{285} I'm known for making movies
But I also have a theme park
from Star Wars to Marvel
I'm collecting your favorite things
When I'm not creating them

{286} If I told you, you were a wizard
On your 11th birthday, then
I bet you would know, and have had adventures
Over the next number of years
You spend at school

287
I am another movie, though
You've watched me on the inside
But i'm only trying to show
What happens on the outside

288
If you were surrounded
By monstrous beasts
But instead of killing them
You'd ask them to join in a feast
Well maybe you're likely to train
Them, and fly with them at least.

289
If you were to start liking me, but then after the movie, you split
Never texting me back again
That you did this to me, try to admit it

290
If perhaps you saw me in life
At an all-time low. My hair disheveled
My proportions awkward but then i start to grow

And all of a sudden years later you see me _____

291
I'm not referring to a captain
Nor am i referring to a hat
In fact, i'm what you say
When you're being fully honest

You may say _____ _____

292
You may have heard of me
In *Indiana Jones*, or perhaps
In a dance move when I say
Watch me, watch me

293
A game on a mobile phone
Where you discover who did it
As you're moving about beware
I may have more crimes to commit
Hopefully, you catch me or prepare
Your ship

294
I'm not sure what's all the fuss
When you see me acting dubious

You may say i'm acting _____

295
I'll take you on an apocalyptic adventure
As my family drives around the screen
We may struggle to get along
But we have power as a dysfunctional team
A movie that shows a family can be strong

296
All we do is sit and wait
As we draw cute kittens
But eventually someone's fate
Involves exploding their mittens
What game are we playing?

297
If you were to hear what i've spoken
About the longtime problems we face

You might say "whoa man you're _____"
On issues like philosophy and race

298 Fire, Water, Earth, and Air
Too much time has passed
And now you must prepare
To face the evil of the past
A young child's burden to bear

299 You watched Back to the future when you were bored,
You'd say they almost have it right

Except for our _____ _____
Don't really float or even take flight

300

What music is the couple in the elevator listening to?

✧ Chapter 14: Answers ✦

283. Flossing. First performed in the early 2010s, flossing is a dance move made popular by the 2017 video game Fortnite. Do you know how to floss?

284. Spider webs. *Spider-Man* has been popular since the original comics in the 1960s. You probably know Spider-Man from the more recent film series. Spider Man uses spiderwebs to jump around and between buildings.

285. Disney. Walt Disney is the founder of Disney. He also created the Disney theme parks. Movie franchises like Star Wars and Marvel are owned by Disney.

286. *Harry Potter.* Harry found out he was a wizard when he was 11. After he went off to school at Hogwarts, he had many adventures, some of them quite scary!

287. *Inside Out.* This movie is all about emotions (on the inside) and what they mean in our lives (on the outside).

288. *How to Train your Dragon.* This series of films is all about dragons (monstrous beasts) but the characters in the movies make friends with dragons and work together with them.

289. Ghosting. This term refers to when someone you're dating or hanging out with suddenly stops responding to texts or messages.

290. Glow up. Sometimes as kids and teenagers, we can look and feel quite awkward because we haven't finished growing yet and don't know how best to dress for our own personality. Often when we grow up, we find our best look and get more comfortable in our skin—this is called a "glow up," as over time, we start to look our best.

291. No cap. "Cap" is short for "captain" and is also the name of a type of hat. In this case, "no cap" refers to caps for teeth that can be removed and therefore are considered to be inauthentic (not truthful). "No cap" means that you're speaking the truth.

292. The whip. The title character in *Indiana Jones* carries a stock whip. It also refers to a dance move created by Silentó for his song his "Watch Me (Whip/Nae Nae)," which debuted on May 5, 2015.

293. The Killer Among Us. Also known as "Among Us," this is a murder mystery video game where players have to figure out who did the crime.

294. Sus. Short for "suspicious".

295. *The Mitchells Vs the Machines.* This is a 2021 computer-animated science fiction comedy film about a family on a road trip fighting a robot apocalypse.

296. Exploding Kittens. This is a card game in which players try to avoid getting an exploding kitten card.

297. Woke. This word means being alert to racial prejudice and discrimination. It came from African American Vernacular English (AAVE).

298. *Avatar: the Last Airbender.* This movie tells the story of a young child who has mastered power over fire, water, earth, and air.

299. Hoverboard. This futuristic creation was featured in the movie Back to the Future. Toy hoverboards have been created, but they're not nearly as cool as in our imagination!

300. Elevator music. Yep, this is the music that is played in the elevator.

Chapter 15

Art

✦ Chapter 15: Art ✦

My favorite subject in school is all about Art. I love learning its history as well as new techniques and mediums that I can try. Enjoy these next riddles which are all about art.

 301
Most known for my smile
And on the wall of the louvre
A man known for dreaming of flight
Painted me not knowing the world
Would make such ado

 302
Painted by someone who never knew
The talent that they had or the fame
They would receive after they left that would ensue
A simple painting outside my window frame
As i sit in my asylum, in pain having no clue

I paint the _____ _____

 303
I am one of seven elements of art
If you take me at a point and draw me very fine,
Straight through the picture, you start
To draw a point that creates a path, put simply a _____

 304
Perhaps you've taken all your favorite things
As pictures cut and pasted you add them
To your locker, to your folder, to your room
The common theme they hold is often where they stem
From when you're making one of me
What art form do i describe?

305
The same artist as 301 painted me,
A meal shared by well-known men,
A figure at its center

306
You see him reaching out
You see omnipotence reaching down
This moment goes back to genesis
The story of creation is found

307
Three ships moving toward me
You see Mount Fuji in the back
My greatest element is my name
See if you can say it back

308
I am the artist of 302
Though this is a picture of myself
Therefore, the name is that of me
And then that of myself

309
I'm where originally depicted 306 exists
If you stare straight up at the ceiling
You will find that i am hard to miss
You will have a grand wondrous feeling
As you see me painted by michelangelo

310
An artist known in the streets
However, the artist remains unknown
A young child holding something she can't eat
But in order to make it, it had to be blown
A symbol, some say, of lost innocence

311

What do you perceive on the surface
Is it rough, is it smooth? How have my lines
Defined it, does it serve a purpose
This aspect is real but more likely visual
When i add hair to the dog or wrinkles to the woman

I am adding _____

312

If I am not real then I am?

313

If you met me, you'd say David
You are such a Great Thinker
Even Apollo and Daphne agree
But perhaps The Motherland Calls you
To rediscover The Great Sphinx of Giza
Before you finish making me,
What am I?

314

If you took your art outside
Then you took into account the light
And though you painted almost realness
You left quite the impression
What style are you painting in?

315

If you were to accurately and honestly
Represent the world. Such as painting
That bowl of fruit. With as much pains taking
Detail as you possibly could then would

Might say that you are painting _____

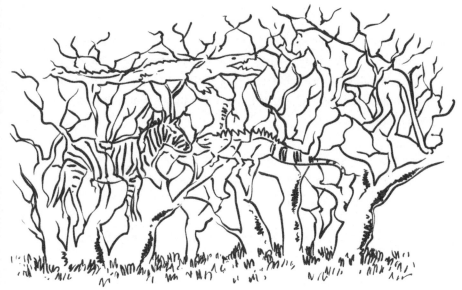

1ˢᵗ riddle question: How many animals do you see?

2ⁿᵈ riddle question: What significance do these animals hold in this book?

✦ *Chapter 15: Answers* ✦

301. Mona Lisa. This painting hangs in the art gallery in Paris called the Louvre. It's a painting of a woman smiling. The painter of this artwork, Leonardo Da Vinci, was also known for his inventions, including ideas for flying machines. When he painted the Mona Lisa, he had no idea that is would become so famous after his death.

302. The Starry Night. The creator of this artwork, Van Gogh, did not know fame during his lifetime. Van Gogh painted this masterpiece while staying at an asylum (due to mental health problems).

303. Line. This is one of the seven elements of art. It seems basic, but you can sure do a lot with lines!

304. Collage. This type of art combines lots of different images all pasted together. It's a popular art form for decorating daily items with a personal touch. Sometimes a collage can make a larger picture from many smaller ones, such as a self portrait.

305. The Last Supper. Leonardo Da Vinci also painted this artwork. It represents the scene of the Last Supper of Jesus with the Twelve Apostles, from The Bible. The figure at the centre of the painting is Jesus.

306. The Creation of Adam. "Omnipotence" means "the quality of having unlimited or great power." Gods are often said to be omnipotent. This painting by Michelangelo is of a scene from the Book of Genesis in The Bible, in which God reaches down to Adam, who he has created.

307. The Great Wave of Kanagawa. This painting shows a giant wave with Japan's Mount Fuji in the background. Have you seen this famous image on t-shirts and other decorative items?

308. Van Gogh Self Portrait. This is a painting that Van Gogh did of himself and named after himself!

309. Sistine Chapel Ceiling. The Sistine Chapel Ceiling is where the Creation of Adam was originally painted. It is one of the most amazing artworks in the world, that evokes (causes) feelings of wonder in those who view it.

310. Girl with Balloon by Banksy. Banksy is a street artist, which means he makes art in urban environments, such as on the walls of buildings. No one knows who Banksy is!

311. Texture. Texture can refer to how something feels but also how this is shown in painted works of art.

312. Abstract.

313. Sculpture. The clues refer to famous works of sculpture.

314. Impressionism. This is a 19th-century art movement that put emphasis on accurately showing light in its changing qualities to create a sense of reality

315. Realism. This is a mid-19th-century artistic movement in which subjects were painted from everyday life in a realistic way.

316. There are four animals. An alligator, iguana, zebra, and jaguar. Answer B. The first letter of each of these animals is the same as the first name of each of the kids introduced in this book.

Chapter 16

Space

✦✦ Chapter 16: Space ✦✦

> My favorite subject by far has everything to do with outer space. I hope to be able to travel outside earth's atmosphere someday. Where do I want to travel to?

317

I am something in the sky
That seems to shine at night
However, I'm not a star
I am Earth's satellite

318

The closest planet to our own
Though the hottest in our system
Where a day is longer than a year

319

You can't really put a ring on me
For i already have seven created
From a cataclysmic event you see
Where part of the debris vacated

320

A man was just doing his job,
When his suit was torn.
Why did he die three minutes later?

321

As I Sojourn through these rocks
I say this is my Opportunity to act with Spirit,
Curiosity, and Perseverance
What am I?

186,000 miles in a second
Is how fast that i can go.
If you went that fast then
You could say you're traveling

At the _____ _____ _____

 There was a war though it was very cold
It involved exploring a whole new world
But who got there first mattered, to be bold
And remembered forever as the first who entered
The world that swirled up above
What am i describing?

 First part millions in our sky,
Second part thousands on our planet
Equals a series that has spanned generations

 I'm at the beginning of the end and the start of eternity,
At the end of time and space, in the middle of yesterday
But nowhere in tomorrow. What am i?

 I am not a cowboy but my best friend is
I am not a hero but i am a toy

 I am moving constantly
Round and round i go
So, when you look at me,
No patterns will start to show

I have keys but no locks. I have a space but no room.
You can enter, but can't go outside. What am i?

 I am the study of the stars
And all the planets that you see
And cannot see. But even though
You don't see me you can still study me

 When you see me, i seem large
But i'm most in use once i'm really small
The power it takes to propel me to move
At the start is different from the rest
So please ensure i don't fail to launch
Or i'll never get to where i want to go

 You are held down by me
My weight ever upon you
If you were to jump, i'd push
You back down, only on the moon,
Would i not push you around
So hard.

 I have been followed for centuries
As you place your hands up to the sky
And follow with all your heart
In order to cross the terrible sea
And get to where you need to be

What is at the center of the black hole?

✧ *Chapter 16: Answers* ✷

317. Moon.

318. Venus. Yep, a day in Venus lasts longer than an Earth year!

319. Saturn. Saturn has seven rings that were created by bits and pieces of colliding moons.

320. Because he was an astronaut

321. A Space rover—rovers make their way through the rocks of the planets and the riddle also names five rovers on Mars.

322. Speed of Light.

323. Space Race. The race to get into space was a major event of the 20th century, with different countries trying to be the first!

324. Star Wars. This refers to the famous film series set in space that is beloved by people of all ages.

325. The letter E. Eternity starts with the letter E, and when you say it out loud it ends with an "E" sound. The words "time" and "space" both end in E, and it's in the middle of the word "yesterday." There's no E in the word "tomorrow"

326. Buzz Lightyear. This is a character from the movie Toy Story. His best friend is a cowboy named Woody.

327. Constellations.

328. A keyboard. The buttons on a keyboard are called "keys." A keyboard has a "space" bar and an "enter" key.

329. Astronomy. You can use a telescope and images from outer space to study the planets and stars that you can't see from Earth with the naked eye (that means, with your eyes only!).

330. Rocket. As a rocket takes off, it sheds its parts, making it smaller as it goes up. The moment of launch is very important—if it fails to get enough power, the rocket won't go anywhere!

331. Gravity. The theory of gravity explains why we all don't just float away

332. North Star. The North Star has been used by humans throughout history to navigate, including at sea.

333. The letter E. Riddle 325 answer is the letter E. The letters in the puzzle make up the word Letter then at the center of the hole would be the answer to 325, which is an E.

✧ Conclusion ✧

Thank you for solving our riddles! We hope you enjoyed going on a journey to discover where we are from! And what we enjoy doing!

If you enjoyed solving our riddles, why not try to make a riddle of your own? Start with a subject that you enjoy!

Then find words that have double meanings.

Or make a fun rhyme about something that you like.

You can even come up with an answer first and see if you can make a riddle out of the answer.

The best part is getting friends and family to try to solve your riddles! So, until next time, keep solving riddles and having fun!

Printed in Great Britain
by Amazon

33362631R00076